RATTLESNAKES

by Sophie Lockwood

Content Adviser: Harold K. Voris, PhD, Curator and Head,
Amphibians and Reptiles, Department of Zoology,
The Field Museum, Chicago, Illinois

THE CHILD'S WORLD®, CHANHASSEN, MINNESOTA

RATTLESNAKES

Published in the United States of America by The Child's World®
PO Box 326 • Chanhassen, MN 55317-0326 • 800-599-READ • www.childsworld.com

Acknowledgements:

The Child's World®: Mary Berendes, Publishing Director

Editorial Directions, Inc.: E. Russell Primm, Editorial Director; Pam Rosenberg, Editor; Judith Shiffer, Assistant Editor; Caroline Wood and Rory Mabin, Editorial Assistants; Susan Hindman, Copy Editor; Emily Dolbear and Sarah E. De Capua, Proofreaders; Elizabeth Nellums, Olivia Nellums, and Daisy Porter, Fact Checkers; Tim Griffin/IndexServ, Indexer; Cian Loughlin O'Day, Photo Researcher, Linda S. Koutris, Photo Editor

The Design Lab: Kathleen Petelinsek, Art Director and Cartographer; Julia Goozen, Page Production Artist

Photos:

Cover: Tom Ulrich / Stone / Getty Images; frontispiece / 4: Siede Preis / Photodisc / Getty Images.

Interior: Alamy Images: 5-bottom left and 34 (Byron Jorjorian), 24 (John Cancalosi / Peter Arnold Inc.), 36 (Kike Calvo / Visual and Written SL); Animals Animals / Earth Scenes: 12 (Paul & Joyce Berquist), 23 (Zigmund Leszczynski), 33 (Dominique Braud); Ben Chrisman / The Daily Times / AP Photo: 27; Corbis: 5-top right and 16 (David A. Northcott), 5-bottom right and 29 (Bowers Museum of Cultural Art); Joe McDonald / Corbis: 5-middle and 21, 15, 18, 30; Papilio / Alamy Images: 5-top left and 9 (Robert Pickett), 11 (Jack Milchanowski); Adalberto Rios Szalay / Sexto Sol / Photodisc / Getty Images: 2-3.

Library of Congress Cataloging-in-Publication Data

Lockwood, Sophie.
  Rattlesnakes / by Sophie Lockwood.
    p. cm. — (The world of reptiles)
  Includes bibliographical references (p.   ) and index.
  ISBN 1-59296-549-0 (library bound : alk. paper)
  1. Rattlesnakes—Juvenile literature. I. Title.
  QL666.O69L63 2006
  597.96'38—dc22   2005024791

TABLE OF CONTENTS

Chapter One

On the Prairie's Edge

It is April in Alberta, Canada. The last snows are melting, and snakes awaken deep in a prairie dog's burrow. Four species of snakes **hibernated** together all winter. Large, thick-bodied prairie rattlesnakes account for the majority of snakes. But bull snakes, blue racers, and garter snakes join the rattlers each winter. Slowly, spring warmth fills the den, and the snakes begin to emerge—more than 400 sluggish, hungry, squirming snakes. Most **denning** groups have 250 snakes or so. Really large dens may have 500 snakes. They slither out of their hideaway like spaghetti being poured from a pot.

Prairie rattlesnakes usually return to the same den each October. Several generations—from **juveniles** to great-grandparents—will hibernate together through the winter. After six months of sleep, the snakes pour out of the den. They lie in the sun near the den to warm their bodies. Rattlesnakes are reptiles and cannot create their

Prairie Rattlesnake Fast Facts
(Crotalus viridis)
Adult length: 35 to 45 inches
   (89 to 114 centimeters)
Coloration: Gray-green bodies
   with greenish splotches
Range: North American mixed
   grass and shortgrass prairies
Reproduction: Live births of 7
   to 13 young
Diet: Mice, rats, gophers, ground
   birds, toads, frogs, lizards, and
   baby burrowing owls

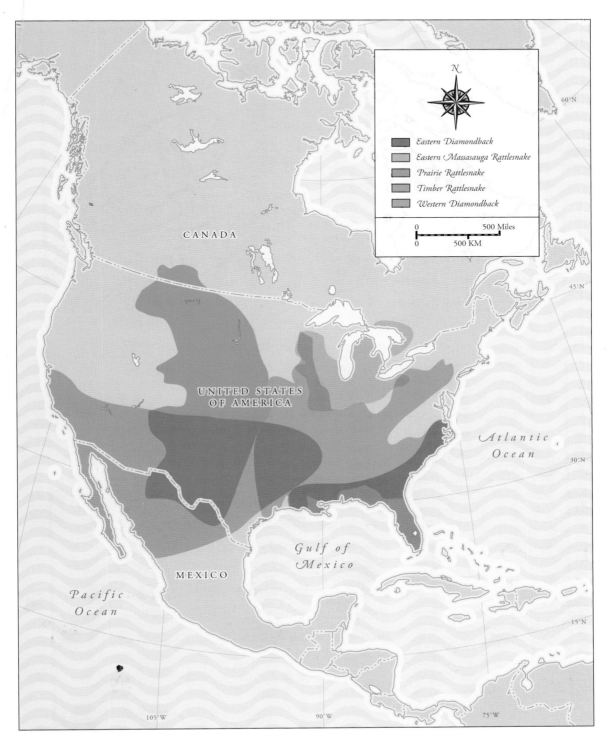

This map shows the habitats of select rattlesnake species of North America.

own body heat. They rely on the sun to warm them up and get them moving.

April to October is an active time for the rattlers. Once they have warmed up enough, they leave the den area in search of food. Prairie rattlesnakes may eat two or three times their own weight between April and October. Meals are small—a couple of ounces at most—so that means many meals are required.

The prairie land comes alive through spring and summer. Wheatgrass, spear grass, and blue grama grow lush and green in the warm sun. Leafy cottonwoods line the edges of the prairie and dot its water-filled potholes. Scruffy sages form gray-green clusters across the land. Bluebells, columbine, and pink wintergreen dance in the soft prairie breezes.

Springtime also brings out the many animals that have survived the long winter. Grasshoppers, worms, spiders, ground beetles, and flies mate and produce eggs. Birds build nests, lay eggs, and feed their chicks the insects flying and crawling through the prairie grasses. Mice, gophers, prairie dogs, and ground squirrels give birth to litters of young.

Small creatures attract **predators,** such as coyotes, hawks, owls, and rattlesnakes. Some predators hunt in the day, when excellent vision comes in handy. Prairie

rattlesnakes prefer the night. They are members of the pit viper family and have heat sensors in pits between their eyes and nostrils.

When night comes, many rodents scavenge for food. They do not see the deadly rattlesnake that waits motionless for its prey. The snake tastes the air. Its heat sensors identify the body heat of a ground squirrel. Sensors pinpoint the prey's exact size and location. The rattler strikes, and **venom** enters the ground squirrel's body. The squirrel tries to run, but dies within a few yards. The snake follows close behind. It turns the squirrel headfirst and swallows it whole.

This is nature on the prairie. Plants feed some animals. Insects feed others. Larger animals eat the smaller ones. And, when the larger ones die, their decaying bodies feed insects and nourish the soil so that bluebells and columbine can grow again.

The prairie rattlesnake can be found in the Great Plains region of the United States, in southern Alberta, Canada, and northern Mexico.

Did You Know?
The Lakota people call the prairie rattler *sinte hla,* or "rattle tail."

Chapter Two

Beware the Shaking Rattle

Rattlesnakes are reptiles and members of the Viperidae family. They belong to the same snake family as adders, vipers, the feared fer-de-lance, and the deadly bushmaster. Most rattlesnakes have common characteristics: rattles, fangs, and venom.

Rattlesnakes are widespread over North, Central, and South America. Prairie and western rattlers live on the plains in the north. Neotropical rattlesnakes slither through the dry forests of South America, as far south as Argentina. Some rattlers like deserts—Mojaves, western diamondbacks, and sidewinders, for example. Other rattlers—such as timber, Mexican west coast, and canebrakes—prefer forest.

There are two main genera of rattlesnakes: *Crotalus* and *Sistrurus*. *Crotalus* (true rattlesnakes) are medium to large rattlers. They usually have sizable rattles and small

Dusky pygmy rattlesnakes are gray with black spots.
They also have orange spots that run down their backs.

scales covering their heads. The *Sistrurus* species include pygmy rattlesnakes. They are smaller and thinner and have large platelike scales on their heads.

Pygmy rattlers grow to between 15 and 21 inches (38 and 53 cm) long. These rattlers have varied, colorful markings. The largest of the *Sistrurus* snakes is the eastern massasauga rattlesnake that grows to 40 inches (102 cm) long. *Crotalus* rattlesnakes tend to be thicker through the body and longer. The largest species is the eastern diamondback rattlesnake, which can grow up to about 8 feet (2.4 meters) long.

RATTLES

Rattles appear on the tails of all rattlesnake species except one. The Santa Catalina Island rattlesnake has no rattle. Santa Catalinas climb trees and hunt birds. A rattle would be too noisy for a snake sneaking up on a nest of birds.

Instead of a rattle, young rattlers are born with what is called a pre-button. A rattle is produced when the snake sheds its first skin. The rattle grows as the snake

A baby western diamondback rattlesnake has a pre-button instead of a rattle.

Did You Know?
About eight thousand people in the United States receive venomous snakebites each year. Only nine to fifteen of these victims will die. Surprisingly, one-fourth of adult rattlesnake bites carry no venom. Adult snakes control the use and amount of venom in every bite.

grows. The length of the rattle, however, doesn't necessarily show a snake's age. New rattle sections develop with every new skin grown. A well-fed rattler may shed its skin more often than a poorly fed rattler. Also, the rattles are dry, hard sections that can break off as the snake moves over rough land.

Rattles are made up of keratin, the same substance that makes human fingernails and toenails. The sound made is like a bunch of crickets buzzing. Some scientists believe that rattles developed to warn off predators: Don't come after me, I'm dangerous! A good example of this is what happens between bison and western rattlers. The rattles buzz, and the bison move away.

FANGS AND VENOM

A western diamondback rattlesnake waits for a kangaroo rat to pass by. The snake has needle-sharp fangs. When at rest, the fangs fold back against the top of the snake's mouth. Each tooth is hollow like the hypodermic needles that doctors use.

A western diamondback can strike from a distance equal to one-third its body length, about 12 to 15 inches (30 to 38 cm). As it prepares to strike, the snake rears up

on its body, its fangs rotate into place, and its mouth opens very wide. As the fangs pierce the prey's flesh, venom is released from **glands** in the snake's head.

Rattlesnake venom acts in two ways. Some rattlers have venom that acts on the prey's nervous system. Other rattlesnakes make venom that poisons the prey's blood. The venom of most rattlers combines both types. Although rattlesnakes are venomous, there is no poison in their bodies except for in the venom sacs. Many people have eaten rattlesnake meat, and they often say it tastes like chicken.

SPECIAL RATTLESNAKE SENSES

A rattlesnake's sense of smell comes from a special organ in its mouth called the Jacobson's organ. The Jacobson's organ has two highly sensitive hollows, or sacs, in the roof of the mouth that are lined with sensory tissue. This organ improves the snake's sense of smell and allows rattlers to track both prey and future mates.

The Jacobson's organ works together with the snake's forked tongue. The tongue flicks the air. It picks up bits of scent on the air. The brain converts the taste information into usable data—for example, the air

Western Diamondback Rattlesnake Fast Facts

(Crotalus atrox)
Adult length: 3 to 6.5 feet (1 to 2 m)
Coloration: Gray, yellow, pink, or dull red with clear diamond patterns on the back
Range: Southwestern United States and northern Mexico
Reproduction: Live birth of 4 to 25 young
Diet: Rabbits, mice, rats, gophers, sparrows, and ground squirrels

A drop of venom drips from the fang of a diamondback rattlesnake.

tastes like toad, and toad is acceptable food. The rattler ambushes the toad when it hops by.

Like other pit vipers, rattlesnakes also have heat-sensing pits on the sides of their heads that allow them to track prey by their body heat. These sensors are so exact that a snake can detect a tiny mouse from 2 feet (61 cm) away and larger prey from up to 30 feet (9 m) away. The temperature change can be as tiny as one-hundredth of a degree and the snake will still notice the difference.

The combination of taste and heat sensing are excellent detection systems for rattlesnakes. Most rattlers are **nocturnal** and

Rattlesnakes, such as this Mojave rattlesnake, use their tongues along with their Jacobson's organ to detect and identify smells.

often cannot see their prey approaching in the darkness. With taste and heat sensing, rattlers get an accurate idea of the size of the prey and where it is.

PATTERNED SKIN

Rattlesnake skin is made up of overlapping scales. The scales stick out slightly, causing the snake's skin to feel rough to the touch. The bumpy scales protect the snake as it moves over gravel, thornbushes, and other rough surfaces.

Rattlesnakes shed their skins as they grow, just like you get bigger clothes and shoes as you grow. When old skin needs to go, the snake finds something rough to rub against. A stone, a tree stump, or gravel will serve the purpose. During the first year or two, skin is shed about once a month. For adults, skin shedding may happen once a year. Snakes that grow faster need to shed their skins more often.

Skin covers the snake's eyes, as well as its body. Over time, the eye covering is scratched. When the snake's skin peels off, the eyes get a new covering. For a while, the snake cannot see well. During this time, the rattler could easily fall prey to one of its many predators. Right after shedding, a sensible rattler hides until its full vision returns.

Chapter Three

Chipmunk for Dinner

A male timber rattler slips through the rubble of a western New York forest. He is only a short distance from his winter den. Most rattlers never travel more than a couple of miles from their denning site. This male is a large snake, slightly more than 4 feet (1.2 m) long. He is yellowish brown with dark brown bands on his body and a black tail. A tan rattle marks him as a rattlesnake.

It is sunset, and the timber rattler is hunting. He flicks his tongue to taste the air. Chipmunks chatter nearby. The rattler coils his body and waits. Most rattlesnakes prefer ambushing their prey to chasing it. A chipmunk approaches. The timber rattlesnake's coloring blends in with the dead leaves on the forest floor. He is almost invisible. When the chipmunk is 10 inches (25 cm) away, the rattler strikes, injects his venom, then releases his prey.

The chipmunk scurries away but dies a short distance from the snake. The rattler follows its prey by the scent trail it leaves and swallows the dead chipmunk whole. Then the timber rattler slides under a rotting tree

Timber rattlesnakes are found in the forests of eastern North America.

Timber Rattlesnake Fast Facts

(Crotalus horridus)

Adult length: 3 to 6 feet (1 to 1.8 m)

Coloration: Gray or yellowish with black arrowhead shaped markings

Range: Midwestern, eastern, and southeastern United States

Reproduction: Live birth of about 9 young

Diet: Mice, voles, shrews, chipmunks, rabbits, and squirrels

Status: Endangered in parts of its range

stump to rest while his body digests the food.

Rattlesnakes only hunt when they are hungry. The prey on the menu depends on the type of rattler and where it is located. Timber rattlers eat mice, rats, squirrels, chipmunks, voles, and shrews. Mexico's Baja California rattlesnake lives on rodents, lizards, and centipedes. Pygmy rattlesnakes choose mice, lizards, small snakes, and frogs from the wildlife menu. Other rattlesnakes may eat eggs, birds, and insects.

COMBAT DANCE

Male rattlesnakes do not stake out personal territory, although they prefer to be alone. Mating and denning are the only times rattlers come together. In several rattlesnake species, males perform a ritual called combat dancing for the chance to mate.

Two adult males slip toward each other. Their heads are up. They wind the top third or so of their bodies around each other. A great deal of pushing and straining takes places until one snake knocks the other over. Because they are wrapped together, usually both fall over.

Rattlesnakes normally do not use their fangs during the combat dance. Even if they did, there would be no fear of the venom injuring the opponent. Rattlesnakes are safe from their own venom.

The combat dance is repeated over and over until one male gives up. The winner goes along and mates with a female, and the loser retreats.

REPRODUCTION

Female rattlesnakes reach maturity and can reproduce at different ages, depending on the species. Timber rattler females cannot produce young until they are between seven and eleven years old. After giving birth, timber rattler females

Timber rattlesnakes feed on deer mice and other animals.

may not have another litter for three to five years. For prairie rattlesnakes, males become mature at three to four years, while females reach maturity at five years old or older.

For most rattlesnake species, females produce young once every two years. Rattlesnakes are **viviparous.** That means the females give birth to live young. They do not lay eggs.

Baby rattlers are born in a skinlike sac. Newborn snakes measure about 10 inches (25 cm) long. They have fangs, and their venom is as powerful as an adult rattler's venom. The newborns do not have rattles, just buttons on the ends of their tails. Even so, these are full-blooded rattlers, and they have the power-packed bite to prove it.

Once the mother gives birth to her young—usually about ten to a litter—her job is done. She doesn't feed them or help them find food. Newborn rattlesnakes must hunt for themselves. At about one to two weeks old, baby sheds its first skin, and the first section of rattle appears.

WINTER DENNING

In North America, winters are far too cold for rattlesnakes. The farther north the species lives, the earlier the rattler seeks its den. No rattlesnake wants to be caught outside when the first snows fall. From the prairies of Alberta to

A newborn timber rattler is curled up next to its mother.

the northern end of the Baja Peninsula, rattlesnakes seek a warm winter home.

The type of denning site used depends on the rattlesnake species and where it lives. Deep cracks in rocky cliffs, natural caves, and other animals' burrows make acceptable dens. Large, empty prairie dog or badger holes are common dens for prairie rattlers. Western rattlers might prefer a rocky cliff. Western diamondbacks have been known to take over desert tortoise burrows. Once rattlesnakes move in, the previous owner has no desire to return.

The same den is used repeatedly. Scientists have found evidence of dens used every year for a century or more. Mating and birthing usually take place close to the den. In that way, the young can follow their mother's scent into the den when cold weather comes.

Females that are pregnant group together on flat table rocks where the sun can warm them. Some scientists believe that pregnant females do not feed until after their babies are born. Perhaps that is why many rattlers produce young every other year or less frequently. After six months of hibernating without food, what snake would want to go hungry most of the summer, too?

Large groups of rattlesnakes often den together.

Chapter Four

Snake Dances

In the highlands of northern Arizona, members of the Hopi tribe gather. It is time for the annual Hopi Snake Dance. The men wear ceremonial dress. They form a circle and begin to sway, dance, and chant. At first, the chanting is low and rhythmic. The song's volume increases. The music is hymnlike.

After a short time, snakes that have been gathered for the dance slither toward the dancers. The chanting increases in volume and intensity. A Hopi priest picks up a rattlesnake. He bites the snake gently behind the head and dances with the snake in his mouth. Other dancers pick up snakes and dance with them, their outstretched arms holding the snakes high. Not all the snakes are rattlers and not all are venomous.

Slowly, the chanting decreases in intensity. The music becomes slower and quieter. The dancers place the snakes back on the ground, and the snakes slither into the brush beside the clearing.

The Hopi Snake Dance is one of many rituals in which Native Americans honor snakes. Rattlesnakes lived on the land long before Indian tribes moved there. The Hopi have long admired the rattlers' ability to thrive in a harsh environment.

LEGENDS AND MYTHS

There are many legends and myths about rattlesnakes. Louisiana's Chitimacha people tell a myth of two Indians who saved a pair of rattlesnakes in a great flood. After that, the snakes made friends with the humans. They guarded the men's homes when the owners were away,

A Hopi dancer performs a traditional dance.

but departed as soon as the men came home. Those rattlesnakes were most likely eastern diamondback rattlers.

The Cherokee people once believed that if a person reached toward a rattlesnake, and the snake seemed evil and angry, the person would soon die. For the Paiute, a bite by a blind rattlesnake would leave the victim blind as well. The Navajo thought that the soul of an evil man would live on in a rattlesnake.

American Indians made medicines from rattlesnakes and their venom. When Indian guide Sacajawea gave birth to her son on the Lewis and Clark expedition, she was given a brew of water and ground rattlesnake rattle to ease the birth. Folk medicines claimed that dried venom or powdered rattlesnake parts cured skin conditions, diabetes, arthritis, and cancer.

Two rattlesnake remedies were rattlesnake dust and rattlesnake salt. Rattlesnake dust was dried and powdered rattlesnake skin that was used to treat skin ailments. Rattlesnake salt has been made by Latin Americans for many years. A rattlesnake is cut up and placed in a tin of salt. After six months, the dried snake is removed, and the salt is ready to be used. Daily use of rattlesnake salt is supposed to prolong a person's life.

Eastern Diamondback Fast Facts
(Crotalus adamanteus)
Adult length: Up to a maximum of 8 feet (2.4 m)
Coloration: Gray or brown with yellow-framed diamonds centered on the snake's back
Range: Southeastern United States, from the Carolinas to Florida and west to Louisiana
Reproduction: Live births of 8 to 12 young
Diet: Rabbits, squirrels, and birds

SNAKE OIL SALESMEN
AND OTHER ODDITIES

For many years, rattlesnakes have been symbols of good luck—or bad luck—depending on the situation. During

This Native American sculpture of a coiled snake was found in California.

the Revolutionary War, a flag with a rattlesnake bore the slogan Don't Tread on Me. Perhaps the colonial troops were offering their British enemies a warning: Step on us, and we'll bite you.

Gamblers in Wild West saloons often carried bags with rattlesnake rattles in them for good luck. Appalachian fiddlers believed that attaching rattles to their fiddles would help them win fiddling competitions. Either way, the rattles added to the bluegrass music being played.

On the Great Plains, traveling salesmen filled wagons with goods and traveled from town to town. Some of those salesmen sold "rattlesnake oil." They claimed the oil would cure any ailment. It was widely known that these salesmen could not be trusted. Even today, people who make shady deals are sometimes called snake oil salesmen.

Scientists are now testing ways to use rattlesnake venom to cure diseases of the nervous system. Research is under way with people who have permanent nerve damage, such as **paralysis.** Other diseases that might have a snake venom cure are multiple sclerosis (MS) and Alzheimer's disease. It would be a remarkable event if poisonous venom became a lifesaver.

Humans have used rattlesnake rattles as good luck charms and musical instruments.

Chapter Five

Humans and Rattlesnakes

Long ago, the Chippewa Indians of Wisconsin called a snake *massasauga*. The word meant "great river mouth" and referred to the snake known today as the eastern massasauga rattlesnake. This snake is endangered in much of its range, which is the northern plains states eastward to the edge of New York State.

Eastern massasaugas live along riverbanks and in wetland environments. Many people know these dull gray-brown snakes as swamp rattlers. They are members of the genus *Sistrurus*. Massasaugas are

Eastern Massasauga Rattlesnake Fast Facts
(Sistrurus catenatus)
Adult length: 18 to 40 inches (46 to 102 cm)
Coloration: Gray or brownish-gray with dark hourglass-shaped markings
Range: Midwestern to eastern United States and Canada
Reproduction: Live birth of 3 to 20 young
Diet: Shrews, voles, deer mice, small snakes, small frogs, salamanders, toads, and young birds

18 to 40 inches (46 to 102 cm) long. They have five to seven dark bands on their skin and grayish-yellow rattles on their tails.

Loss of habitat has been a serious problem for eastern massasaugas. In the early 1800s, as Milwaukee, Wisconsin, expanded, many rattlers lost their habitats. Farming, city growth, and roads invaded rattlesnake territories. Humans filled in wetlands to use the land for many reasons. In each case, rattlers lost hunting territory and denning sites.

THREATS TO SURVIVAL

Natural threats to survival confront every animal species. Flash floods in the desert, early or late snows on the prairie, and wildfires all impact rattlesnake populations. Their preda-

Eastern massasauga rattlesnakes don't den in groups like many other rattlesnakes. Most massasaugas prefer to den in crayfish burrows.

tors form a surprisingly large group. Wolves, foxes, hogs, raccoons, coyotes, and even skunks prey on rattlesnakes. Bird predators include eagles, hawks, and roadrunners.

The most serious threats, however, come from humans. Part of the problem is a fear of snakes. Rattlesnakes are generally not aggressive. They are shy and retiring and would rather flee than strike. Accidents happen when they are surprised in the wild or when humans tease the snakes.

In the past, many states offered bounties on killing rattlesnakes, causing great damage to rattlesnake populations. A fee was paid for the killing of animals considered to be pests, such as wolves and rattlesnakes. Hunters caught and killed rattlers at their denning sites. Several hundred rattlers could be captured at one time, and the hunters collected five dollars per skin. The bounty was stopped in 1975. At that time, the eastern massasauga rattler was placed on Wisconsin's endangered species list.

In states where corn and wheat are grown, killing rattlesnakes proved to be costly. Grains attract rats and mice. Rattlesnakes, which eat rats and mice, are nature's mousetraps, and are far more efficient at their jobs than anything humans have invented. One rattlesnake takes the place of pounds of pesticides, or poisons, sprayed on grain to kill rodents.

Most rattlers are shy and will not strike humans unless surprised or teased.

Even today, fairs in the Midwest and West offer rattlesnake skins, rattles, hatbands, belts, and boots for sale. Rattler meat is roasted and sold as snacks. TRAFFIC, a wildlife trade watchdog organization, reports that about 125,000 rattlesnakes a year are killed for their skins, meat, and gallbladders. The gallbladders are used to make traditional Asian folk medicines.

RECOVERY PROGRAMS

Zoos have become active in conserving rattlesnakes. Their exhibits and **conservation** presentations help people

A Southern Pacific rattlesnake is handled by a zookeeper. Many zoos are working to increase the numbers of endangered rattlesnakes.

learn about rattlesnakes. The hope is that understanding rattlesnakes will make them less threatening. People will know what to do when they meet snakes in the wild—other than chopping them up with the side of a shovel.

Captive breeding programs offer two opportunities to save the snakes. First, they supply rattlesnakes for other zoos so that fewer snakes are taken from the wild. Second, they may be released to strengthen population numbers of rattlesnakes in the wild.

Most rattlesnake species have a slow reproductive cycle. Females must be at least five years old before breeding. Then they breed only every two, three, or more years. For a timber rattler, a female may only produce three or four litters during her lifetime. Juvenile rattlers have a high death rate. They become prey to many species.

By breeding snakes in zoos, the high death rate is overcome. Zoo specialists raise the juveniles to adult age. They keep 90 percent of juveniles alive, as opposed to juvenile death rates of 90 to 95 percent for rattler species in the wild. Even with captive breeding, recovery of a species such as timber rattlers or massasaugas may take decades. Let's hope they survive that long.

Glossary

conservation (kon-sur-VAY-shuhn) the act of saving or preserving some aspect of wildlife

denning (DEN-ing) spending the winter in a den

glands (GLANDZ) organs that produce chemical substances or let other substances leave the body

hibernated (HYE-bur-nate-ed) slept for a long period through the winter

juveniles (JOO-vuh-nuhlz) youngsters, like human toddlers

nocturnal (nok-TUR-nuhl) active during the night

paralysis (puh-RAL-uh-siss) an inability to move one or more parts of the body

predators (PRED-uh-turz) animals that hunt and kill other animals for food

venom (VEN-uhm) poison produced by some kinds of snakes and spiders

viviparous (vi-VIP-uh-ruhss) producing young through live births as opposed to eggs

For More Information

Watch It

Nightmares of Nature: Deadly Reptiles. VHS (Washington, D.C., National Geographic, 1997).

Read It

Dewey, Jennifer. *Rattlesnake Dance: True Tales, Mysteries, and Rattlesnake Ceremonies.* Honesdale, Pa.: Boyds Mills Press, 1997.

Durrett, Deanne. *Rattlesnakes.* San Diego: Kidhaven Press, 2004.

Wechsler, Doug. *Rattlesnakes.* New York: PowerKids Press, 2001.

Look It Up

Visit our home page for lots of links about rattlesnakes: *http://www.childsworld.com/links*

Note to Parents, Teachers, and Librarians: We routinely verify our Web links to make sure they are safe, active sites—so encourage your readers to check them out!

The Animal Kingdom
Where Do Rattlesnakes Fit In?

Kingdom: Animal

Phylum: Chordata

Class: Reptilia

Order: Squamata

Family: Viperidae

Genus: *Crotalus* or *Sistrurus*

Species: There are about 30 species of rattlesnakes

Index

About the Author

Sophie Lockwood is a former teacher and a longtime writer. She writes textbooks, newspaper articles, and magazine articles. Sophie enjoys writing about animals and their habits. The most interesting part of her research, Sophie says, is learning how scientists apply their knowledge to save endangered species. She lives with her husband in the foothills of the Blue Ridge Mountains.